PRESENTED TO

_____

BY

_____

FaithWords
Hachette Book Group
1290 Avenue of the Americas, New York, NY 10104
faithwords.com
twitter.com/faithwords

First Edition: February 2019

FaithWords is a division of Hachette Book Group, Inc. The FaithWords name and logo are
trademarks of Hachette Book Group, Inc.

The publisher is not responsible for websites (or their content) that are not owned by the publisher.

The Hachette Speakers Bureau provides a wide range of authors for speaking events. To find out
more, go to www.hachettespeakersbureau.com or call (866) 376-6591.

Print book interior design and layout by Koechel Peterson & Associates.

ISBNs: 978-1-5460-3600-5 (paper over board), 978-1-5460-1398-3 (ebook)

Printed in the United States of America

LSC-C

10 9 8 7 6 5 4 3 2 1

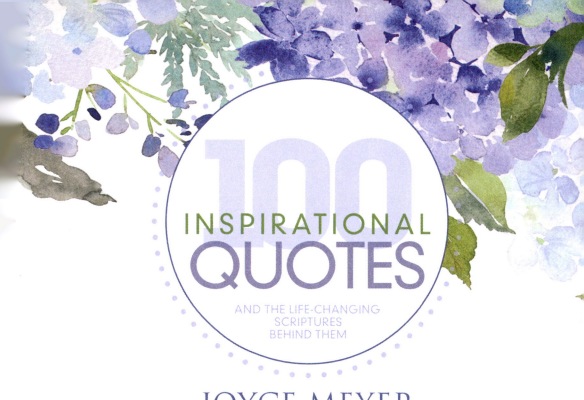

100 INSPIRATIONAL QUOTES

AND THE LIFE-CHANGING SCRIPTURES BEHIND THEM

JOYCE MEYER

Throughout
the forty plus
years

that I've been privileged to teach God's Word, He has given me ways to communicate biblical principles so that they really strike a chord with people. It's so exciting when this happens because my life's goal is to help people understand the Bible and learn how to apply it to their lives, and my prayer is this book will help you do just that!

As you read it, you'll find brief points God has given me in my teachings that you can easily take in and think about as you go through your day. Each quote has an accompanying Scripture verse (or verses) that gives the biblical truth behind it. This is important because it's the Truth God gives us that makes a life-changing difference—not the thoughts or opinions of another person.

My hope is that you will use this resource to help keep your mind focused on God and His Word; it could also be a starting point for a Bible study. Maybe you not only need a brief word of encouragement, but some direction to go deeper in what God has to say about a challenging situation you're facing. You can take the key scripture listed with the quote that inspires you and do key word studies of terms in the verse or look up other verses that speak to the topic in a concordance. I also want to encourage you to pray as you meditate on the Word, asking the Holy Spirit to teach you what you need to know. He is THE Teacher, as John 14:26 tells us.

Keep God first in everything you do and every part of your life. He loves you and always has your best interest at heart. Trust Him to guide you through His Word in your everyday life, and you'll enjoy your journey!

Joyce

Where the **MIND** goes, the **MAN** follows.

"For as he thinks
in his heart,
so is he..."

PROVERBS 23:7 NKJV

*"Do not conform
to the pattern of this world,
but be transformed
by the renewing of your mind.
Then you will be able to test
and approve what God's will is—
his good, pleasing and perfect will."*

ROMANS 12:2 NIV

YOU CAN CHANGE YOUR LIFE BY LETTING THE WORD OF GOD CHANGE YOUR MIND.

God doesn't just give you the dream; HE GIFTS YOU THE FAITH TO BELIEVE IT!

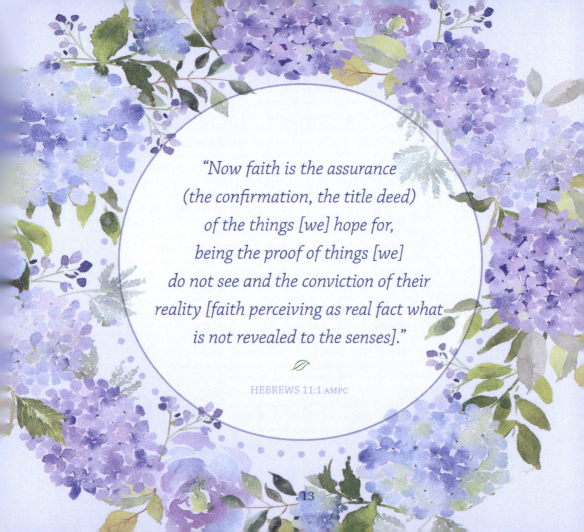

"Now faith is the assurance
(the confirmation, the title deed)
of the things [we] hope for,
being the proof of things [we]
do not see and the conviction of their
reality [faith perceiving as real fact what
is not revealed to the senses]."

HEBREWS 11:1 AMPC

13

In your journey
with Jesus,
YOUR WORST DAY WITH HIM
WILL ALWAYS BE BETTER THAN
your best day
without Him.

"For a day in Your courts
is better than a thousand [anywhere else];
I would rather stand [as a doorkeeper]
at the threshold
of the house of my God
than to live [at ease] in the tents
of wickedness."

PSALM 84:10

I may NOT be
where I need to be,
but thank God
I'm NOT
where I used to be.

I'M OKAY
and I'm on my way!

"And we all…
continually seeing as in a mirror
the glory of the Lord,
are progressively being transformed
into His image from [one degree of]
glory to [even more] glory,
which comes from the Lord,
[who is] the Spirit."

2 CORINTHIANS 3:18

"This is how God showed his love
among us: He sent his one
and only Son into the world
that we might live through him.
This is love: not that we loved God,
but that he loved us and sent his Son
as an atoning sacrifice for our sins."

1 JOHN 4:9-10 NIV

I don't need to do
SOMETHING
IMPORTANT
TO BE IMPORTANT;
I am important
because God loves me
and He sent
Jesus to die for me.

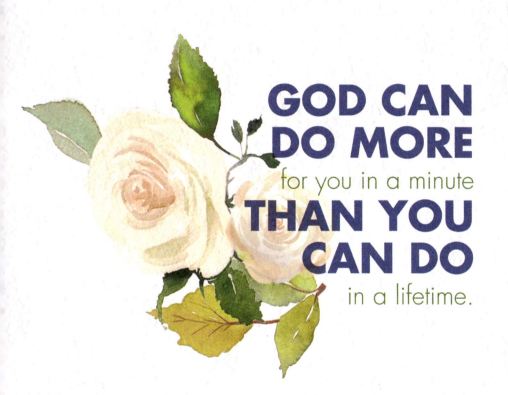

GOD CAN DO MORE for you in a minute **THAN YOU CAN DO** in a lifetime.

"Now all glory to God,

who is able,

through his mighty power at work within us,

to accomplish infinitely more

than we might ask or think."

EPHESIANS 3:20 NLT

WE GET INTO TROUBLE
when we start
EXPECTING
PEOPLE
to do for us what
ONLY GOD
CAN DO.

"'The Lord is my portion,'

says my soul,

'Therefore I hope in Him!'"

LAMENTATIONS 3:24 NKJV

God created us to please Him,

WHICH SETS US FREE
FROM THE NEED TO PLEASE PEOPLE.

Be a God-pleaser,

NOT A PEOPLE-PLEASER.

"Am I now trying to win the favor and approval of men, or of God?
Or am I seeking to please someone?
If I were still trying to be popular with men,
I would not be a bond servant of Christ"

GALATIANS 1:10

"Let us then approach
God's throne of grace with confidence,
so that we may receive mercy
and find grace
to help us in our time of need."

HEBREWS 4:16 NIV

ALWAYS

GO TO GOD FIRST
WHEN YOU HAVE A PROBLEM.

GO TO
THE
THRONE,

NOT THE PHONE.

"And He said to me,
'My grace is sufficient for you,
for My strength is made perfect in weakness.'
Therefore most gladly I will
rather boast in my infirmities,
that the power of Christ may rest upon me."

✠ | CORINTHIANS 12:9 NKJV

STOP TRYING TO
GIVE GOD
EVERYTHING
YOU ARE
AND
START GIVING HIM
EVERYTHING
YOU ARE NOT.
HIS STRENGTH
IS MADE PERFECT
IN OUR WEAKNESS!

Remember
God is not surprised
by your faults.
He knew about them
before you did,
and He loves you
anyway!

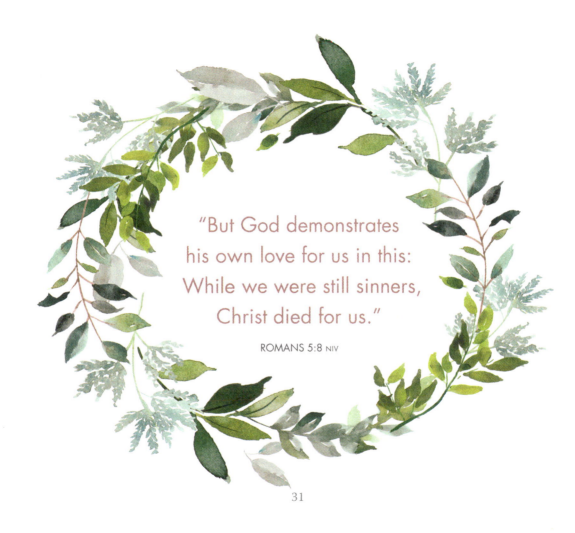

"But God demonstrates his own love for us in this: While we were still sinners, Christ died for us."

ROMANS 5:8 NIV

We don't need SELF-CONFIDENCE; we need GOD-CONFIDENCE.

"*Everything else is worthless*
when compared with the infinite value
of knowing Christ Jesus my Lord.
For his sake I have discarded everything else,
counting it all as garbage,
so that I could gain Christ and become one with him.
I no longer count on my own righteousness
through obeying the law;
rather, I become righteous through faith in Christ..."

PHILIPPIANS 3:8-9 NLT

NEW LEVEL

NEWDEVIL!

*"For a wide door of opportunity
for effectual [service] has opened to me
[there, a great and promising one],
and [there are] many adversaries."*

1 CORINTHIANS 16:9 AMPC

We need to
take God out of our
"emergency only"
box and allow Him
into our
everyday life.

"Trust in and rely confidently on the Lord with all your heart and do not rely on your own insight or understanding. In all your ways know and acknowledge and recognize Him, and He will make your paths straight and smooth..."

PROVERBS 3:5-6

"Get wisdom,
get understanding;
 do not forget my words
 or turn away from them.
Do not forsake wisdom,
and she will protect you;
 love her, and she will
 watch over you."

PROVERBS 4:5-6 NIV

WISDOM MEANS DOING NOW WHAT YOU WILL BE HAPPY WITH LATER ON.

Be determined to discipline yourself to do what's right— no matter how you feel, what you think or what everybody else is doing.

"Now every athlete who [goes into training and]
competes in the games is disciplined
and exercises self-control in all things.
They do it to win a crown that withers,
but we [do it to receive] an imperishable
[crown that cannot wither]."

1 CORINTHIANS 9:25

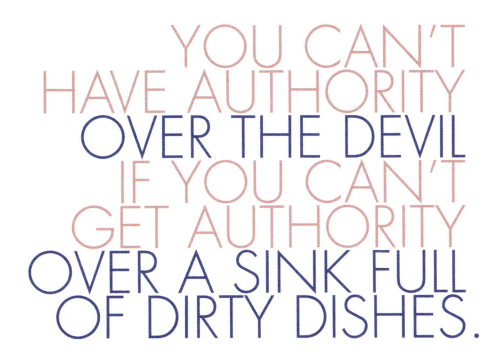

YOU CAN'T HAVE AUTHORITY OVER THE DEVIL IF YOU CAN'T GET AUTHORITY OVER A SINK FULL OF DIRTY DISHES.

YOU CAN FEEL 'WRONG' AND STILL DO WHAT'S RIGHT. START CHOOSING TO DO WHAT YOU KNOW IS RIGHT AND EVENTUALLY YOUR FEELINGS WILL CATCH UP.

"Do not let sin control the way you live;
do not give in to sinful desires.
Do not let any part of your body become
an instrument of evil to serve sin.
Instead, give yourselves completely to God,
for you were dead,
but now you have new life.
So use your whole body as an instrument
to do what is right for the glory of God."

ROMANS 6:12-13 NLT

Don't mourn
bad decisions;
OVERCOME THEM
WITH GOOD ONES.

"I call heaven and earth
as witnesses against you today,
that I have set before you life and death,
the blessing and the curse;
therefore, you shall choose life
in order that you may live,
you and your descendants."

DEUTERONOMY 30:19

*"But you, O Lord, are a God
of compassion and mercy,
slow to get angry
and filled with unfailing love
and faithfulness."*

PSALM 86:15 NLT

There is never

ONE
MOMENT

in your life when God

DOESN'T

love you!

Expect something good to happen to you today!

"Therefore the Lord waits [expectantly]
and longs to be gracious to you,
and therefore He waits on high to have compassion on you.
For the Lord is a God of justice,
blessed (happy, fortunate) are all those
who long for Him [since He will never fail them]."

ISAIAH 30:18

Do good works
BECAUSE
you love God,

not to get Him to love you.

"For if you are trying to make yourselves right with God by keeping the law, you have been cut off from Christ! You have fallen away from God's grace. But we who live by the Spirit eagerly wait to receive by faith the righteousness God has promised to us.
For when we place our faith in Christ Jesus, there is not benefit in being circumcised or being uncircumcised. What is important is faith expressing itself in love."

GALATIANS 5:4-6 NLT

ALWAYS VALUE
YOUR REPUTATION
WITH GOD
MORE THAN
YOUR REPUTATION
WITH MAN.

*"For we speak as messengers
approved by God
to be entrusted with the Good News.
Our purpose is to please God,
not people.
He alone examines the motives
of our hearts."*

1 THESSALONIANS 2:4 NLT

"...He who lives in you
is greater (mightier)
than he who is in the world."

———∞∞∞———

1 JOHN 4:4 AMPC

MY ATTITUDE BELONGS TO ME

and I can decide
what it is going to be.

Stop wishing and start pressing.

We don't need more wishbone, we need backbone!

"Finally, be strong in the Lord and in his mighty power.
Put on the full armor of God, so that you can
take your stand against the devil's schemes.
For our struggles is not against flesh and blood,
but against rules, against the authorities,
against the powers of this dark world
and against the spiritual forces
of evil in the heavenly realms."

EPHESIANS 6:10-12 NIV

"I know that there is nothing better
for people than to be happy
and to do good while they live.
That each of them may eat and drink,
and find satisfaction in all their toil—
this is the gift of God."

ECCLESIASTES 3:12-13 NIV

EMBRACE
the season of life you are in
AND SQUEEZE
ALL THE JOY OUT
OF IT THAT YOU CAN.

IF WE TALK TO GOD in the morning **BEFORE WE TALK TO ANYONE ELSE,** we will be a lot easier to get along with.

"Listen to my voice
in the morning, Lord.
Each morning
I bring my requests to you
and wait expectantly."

PSALM 5:3 NLT

THROUGH GOD'S GRACE, WE CAN **LIVE UPRIGHT** INSTEAD OF UPTIGHT.

*"[All] are justified and made upright
and in right standing with God,
freely and gratuitously by His grace
(His unmerited favor and mercy),
through the redemption
which is [provided] in Christ Jesus."*

| ROMANS 3:24 AMPC

*"Those who live according to the flesh
have their minds
set on what the flesh desires;
but those who live in accordance
with the Spirit have their minds
set on what the Spirit desires."*

ROMANS 8:5 NIV

THINK
BEAUTIFUL
THOUGHTS

AND THERE WILL BE NO ROOM

FOR THE
UGLY ONES.

Sometimes
God uses the junk
in other people to
pull the junk
out of you.

"Iron sharpens iron;
so a man sharpens
the countenance of his friend
[to show rage
or worthy purpose]."

PROVERBS 27:17 AMPC

WE ONLY HAVE
one life to give
AND WE SHOULD
be careful
WHO AND WHAT
WE GIVE IT TO.

"*Whatever you do [whatever your task my be], work from the soul [that is, put in your very best effort], as [something done] for the Lord and not for men.*"

COLOSSIANS 3:23

"*You, my brothers and sisters,*
were called to be free.
But do not use your freedom
to indulge the flesh;
rather, serve one another
humbly in love."

GALATIANS 5:13 NIV

TRUE FREEDOM IS NOT getting everything you want; IT'S BEING ABLE TO BE HAPPY AND EMOTIONALLY STABLE when you don't get what you want.

"But love [that is, unselfishly seek the best
or higher good for] your enemies,
and do good, and lend, expecting nothing in return;
for your reward will be great (rich abundant),
and you will be sons of the Most High..."

LUKE 6:35

FORGIVE

YOUR ENEMIES QUICKLY.

YOUR ANGER WON'T
CHANGE THEM,
SO WHY BE MISERABLE ALL DAY?
GOD IS YOUR
VINDICATOR!

"For You formed my innermost parts;
You knit me [together] in my mother's womb.
I will give thanks and praise to You,
for I am fearfully and wonderfully made;
wonderful are Your works,
and my soul knows it very well."

PSALM 139:13-14

We are human beings, not human doings.

TO DELIGHT
YOURSELF
IN THE LORD
and let Him give you the desires of your heart
IS MUCH
BETTER THAN
STRUGGLING
while trying to get things for yourself.

*"Delight yourself also in the Lord,
and He will give you the desires
and secret petitions of your heart."*

PSALM 37:4 AMPC

What truly matters in life is WHAT'S HAPPENING IN US, not what's happening around us.

"Let the peace of Christ [the inner calm of one who walks daily with Him] be the controlling factor in your hearts [deciding and settling questions that arise]. To this peace indeed you were called as members in one body [of believers]. And be thankful [to God always]."

COLOSSIANS 3:15

YOU ARE MOST
LIKE GOD
WHEN YOU ARE
GOOD TO THOSE
WHO DON'T
DESERVE IT.

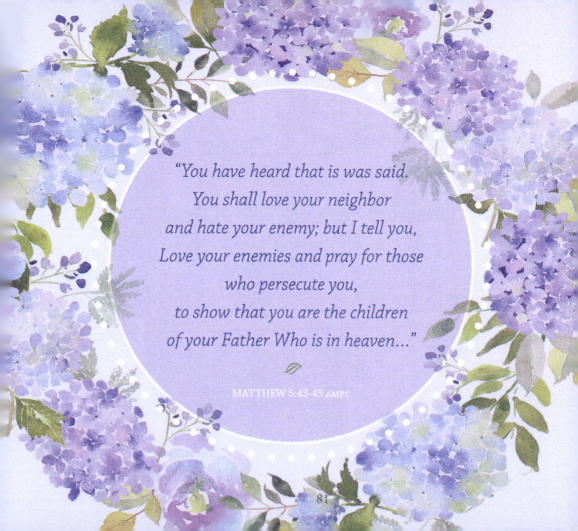

"You have heard that is was said.
You shall love your neighbor
and hate your enemy; but I tell you,
Love your enemies and pray for those
who persecute you,
to show that you are the children
of your Father Who is in heaven..."

MATTHEW 5:43-45 AMPC

"Then they asked Him,
*'What are we to do, so that we
may habitually be doing the
works of God?' Jesus answered,
'This is the work of God: that
you believe [adhere to, trust in,
rely on, and have faith] in the
One whom He has sent.'"*

JOHN 6:28-29

FEAR IS A DEAD END BUT FAITH ALWAYS HAS A FUTURE!

"*I will sing of your strength,*
    in the morning
    I will sing of your love;
    for you are my fortress,
    my refuge in times of trouble.
You are my strength,
    I sing praise to you;
    you, God, are my fortress,
    my God on whom I can rely."

PSALM 59:16-17 NIV

GRATITUDE
IS A GREAT ENERGIZER.
THE MORE
THANKFUL
YOU ARE,
THE BETTER
YOU WILL FEEL!

*"You were taught, with regard to
your former way of life,
to put off your old self, which is being
corrupted by its deceitful desires;
to be made new in the attitude of your
minds; and to put on the new self,
created to be like God in true
righteousness and holiness."*

EPHESIANS 4:22-24 NIV

It isn't what
OTHER PEOPLE
THINK
of us that hurts us—
it's what
WE THINK
of ourselves.

There's nothing better than peace.

Peace equals
more power in your life!

"May the God of your hope
so fill you with all joy and peace in believing
[through the experience of your faith]
that by the power of the Holy Spirit
you may abound and be overflowing
(bubbling over) with hope."

ROMANS 15:13 AMPC

Our lives
are meant
to be SALTY.
THEY SHOULD MAKE
OTHERS THIRSTY
FOR GOD.

*"You are the salt
of the earth..."*

MATTHEW 5:13

PRAY FIRST AND THEN MAKE PLANS.

DON'T PLAN AND THEN PRAY FOR YOUR PLAN TO WORK.

"Be persistent and devoted to prayer,
being alert and focused
in your prayer life
with an attitude of thanksgiving."

COLOSSIANS 4:2

ONE OF THE BEST STATEMENTS
YOU CAN EVER MAKE
IN YOUR RELATIONSHIPS IS:

"I think I'm right but I MAY BE WRONG."

"If possible,

as far as it depends on you,

live at peace with everyone."

ROMANS 12:18

God never asks us
to do anything
WITHOUT
giving us

THE ABILITY
to do it!

"I can do all things
[which He has called me to do]
through Him who strengthens
    and empowers me
[to fulfill His purpose—
I am self-sufficient in Christ's sufficiency;
I am ready for anything
    and equal to anything
    through Him who infuses me
with inner strength and confident peace]."

PHILIPPIANS 4:13

"Who of you by worrying can add one hour to [the length of] his life?"

✝ | MATTHEW 6:27

IT'S OKAY
TO ENJOY YOUR LIFE
WHILE YOU
HAVE A PROBLEM.

BEING MISERABLE
WON'T MAKE
IT GO AWAY
ANY FASTER.

YOU CAN BE
AT PEACE WITH YOUR PAST,
CONTENT WITH YOUR PRESENT,
AND SURE ABOUT YOUR FUTURE',
KNOWING
THAT GOD
LOVES YOU!

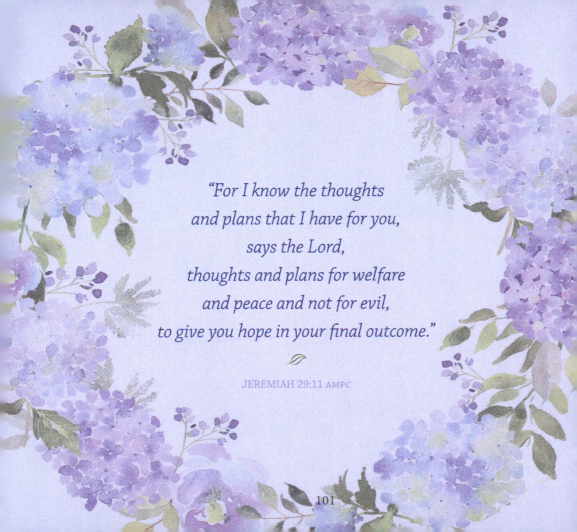

"For I know the thoughts
and plans that I have for you,
says the Lord,
thoughts and plans for welfare
and peace and not for evil,
to give you hope in your final outcome."

JEREMIAH 29:11 AMPC

*"Do nothing from selfishness
or empty conceit
[through factional motives, or strife],
but with [an attitude of] humility
[being neither arrogant nor self-righteous],
regard others as more important
than yourselves."*

PHILIPPIANS 2:3

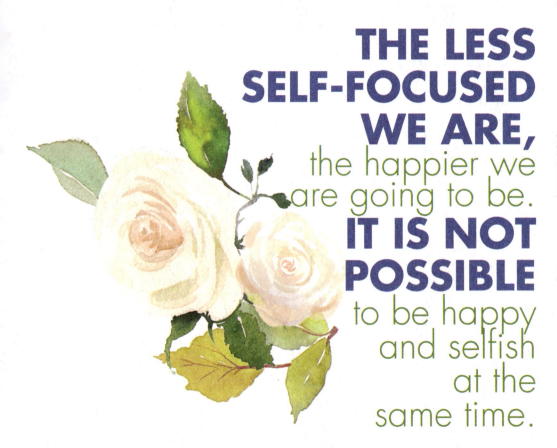

THE LESS SELF-FOCUSED WE ARE, the happier we are going to be. **IT IS NOT POSSIBLE** to be happy and selfish at the same time.

Seek God's face,
not His hand—
who He is,
not just what He
can do for you.

"When You said,
"Seek My face [in prayer,
require My presence
as your greatest need],
my heart said to You,
'Your face, O Lord, I will seek
[on the authority
of Your word]."

PSALM 27:8

WHAT GOD
GIVES ME
BY HIS GRACE IS
HIS GIFT TO ME.
HOW I LIVE MY LIFE
IS MY GIFT
TO GOD.

"I have been crucified with Christ
and I no longer live, but Christ lives in me.
The life I now live in the body,
I live by faith in the Son of God,
who loved me and gave himself for me."

GALATIANS 2:20 NIV

YOU CAN'T
KEEP DOING
THE SAME THING
OVER AND OVER
AND THINK YOU'RE GOING
TO GET A BETTER RESULT.
LET'S LEARN
TO MAXIMIZE OUR LIVES
BY MAXIMIZING OUR TIME.

*"To everything
there is a season,
and a time for every matter
or purpose
under heaven."*

ECCLESIASTES 3:1 AMPC

*"Do not be overcome
and conquered by evil,
but overcome evil with good."*

ROMANS 12:21

Don't waste another day
of your life being angry.
You can
forgive ON PURPOSE,
love ON PURPOSE,
and give ON PURPOSE.
So get happy and do good!

"For it is [not your strength, but it is] God who is effectively at work in you, both to will and to work [that is, strengthening, energizing, and creating in you the longing and the ability to fulfill your purpose] for His good pleasure." PHILIPPIANS 2:13

We have to get over thinking everything should be easy for us. Get rid of the statement

"Its just too hard!"

Because nothing God leads us to do is too hard.

"...Clothe yourselves with humility toward
one another [tie on the servant's apron],
for God is opposed to the proud [the disdainful,
the presumptuous, and He defeats them],
but He gives grace to the humble.
Therefore humble yourselves under
the mighty hand of God [set aside self-righteous pride],
so that He may exalt you [to a place of honor in His service]
at the appropriate time."

1 PETER 5:5-6

YOU CAN BE

PITIFUL
OR
POWERFUL,

BUT CAN'T BE BOTH.

Give up the self-pity and get on with life!

WE CAN'T
CONTROL
WHAT OTHER PEOPLE DO
AND HOW THEY
DECIDE TO TREAT US,
BUT WE CAN
CONTROL
OUR RESPONSE TO THEM.

*"Get rid of all bitterness, rage and anger,
brawling and slander,
along with every form of malice.
Be kind and compassionate to one another,
forgiving each other,
just as in Christ God forgave you."*

EPHESIANS 4:31-32 NIV

JESUS DID NOT DIE TO GIVE US A RELIGION. He died so that through faith in Him, WE COULD HAVE AN INTIMATE RELATIONSHIP WITH GOD.

"...In love He predestined and lovingly planned
for us to be adopted to Himself
as [His own] children through Jesus Christ,
in accordance with the kind intention
and good pleasure of His will."

EPHESIANS 1:4-5

No matter what
you have gone through
or might be going through right now,

you can hope
(have faith) that
God is working
on your behalf right now,
and you will see the results
of His work in your life.

You don't have to be a prisoner
of your circumstances,
but instead you can be

a prisoner
of hope!

"Return to the stronghold
[of security and prosperity],
O prisoners who have the hope;
even today I am declaring that I will restore
double [your former prosperity] to you…"

ZECHARIAH 9:12

*"Let there be no filthiness
and silly talk, or coarse
[obscene or vulgar]
joking, because such things
are not appropriate [for believers];
but instead speak
of your thankfulness [to God]."*

COMPLAINING
keeps us from seeing the
blessings we do have.
GRATITUDE is the
antidote for the poison
of complaining.

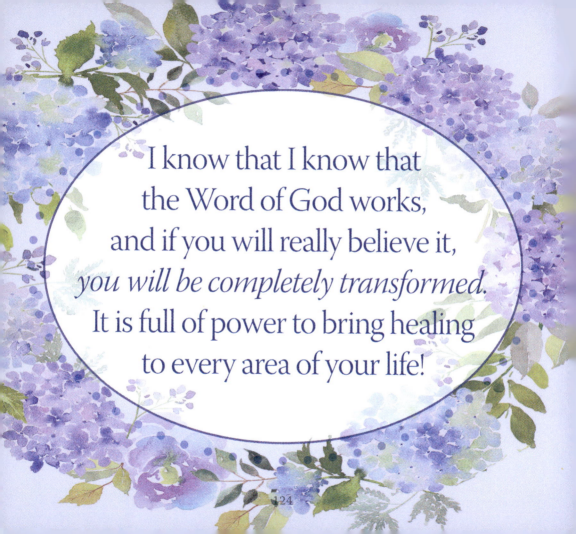

I know that I know that
the Word of God works,
and if you will really believe it,
you will be completely transformed.
It is full of power to bring healing
to every area of your life!

*"All Scripture is inspired by God
and is useful to teach us what is true
and to make us realize what is wrong in our lives.
It corrects us when we are wrong
and teaches us to do what is right.
God uses it to prepare and equip his people
to do every good work."*

2 TIMOTHY 3:16-17 NLT

GOD IS A GIVER,
AND WHEN WE
GIVE
UNSELFISHLY,
we are more like Him
THAN AT ANY OTHER TIME
IN OUR LIVES.

"A new command I give you:

Love one another.

As I have loved you,

so you must love one another."

JOHN 13:34 NIV

Indifference makes
an excuse,
but love
finds a way;
THEREFORE, I REFUSE TO DO NOTHING!

"Righteousness and justice
are the foundation of Your throne;
mercy and loving-kindness
and truth go before Your face."

PSALM 89:14 AMPC

Jesus died for us to have abundant life.

That doesn't mean we won't have any problems; it means there's a place in God where we can live above the problems of life.

*"These things I have spoken to you,
that in Me you may have peace.
In the world you will have tribulation;
but be of good cheer,
I have overcome the world."*

JOHN 16:33 NKJV

JESUS CAME
TO HEAL
THE BROKENHEARTED
AND SET
THE CAPTIVES FREE.
HE CAN
HEAL YOU
EVERYWHERE
YOU HURT!

132

"The Spirit of the Lord God is upon me,
       because the Lord has anointed
       and commissioned me to bring good news
       to the humble and afflicted;
He has sent me to bind up [the wounds of]
       the brokenhearted,
to proclaim release [from confinement and condemnation]
       to the [physical and spiritual]
       captives and freedom to prisoners."

ℭ | ISAIAH 61:1

*"...We also glory in our sufferings,
because we know that suffering
produces perseverance;
perseverance, character;
and character, hope.
And hope does not put us to shame,
because God's love has been poured out
into our hearts through the Holy Spirit,
who has been given to us."*

ROMANS 5:3-5 NIV

Maybe
where you are
right now
is not your fault, but don't let
what happened to you become
an excuse
to stay that way.

"I am the Vine;
you are the branches.
The one who remains in Me
and I in him bears much fruit,
for [otherwise] apart from Me
 [that is, cut off from
  vital union with Me]
you can do nothing."

JOHN 15:5

I'M AN everything-nothing: I'M EVERYTHING with Jesus and NOTHING without Him!

WORDS ARE CONTAINERS FOR POWER.

The power of life and death is in the tongue.

"Death and life
are in the power of the tongue,
and those who love it
and indulge it
will eat its fruit
and bear the consequences
of their words."

PROVERBS 18:21

WE NEED TO MAKE
THE DECISION TO
enjoy every single
day of our lives.
IT'S NOT IRRESPONSIBLE
TO ENJOY YOUR LIFE
while you
have a problem.

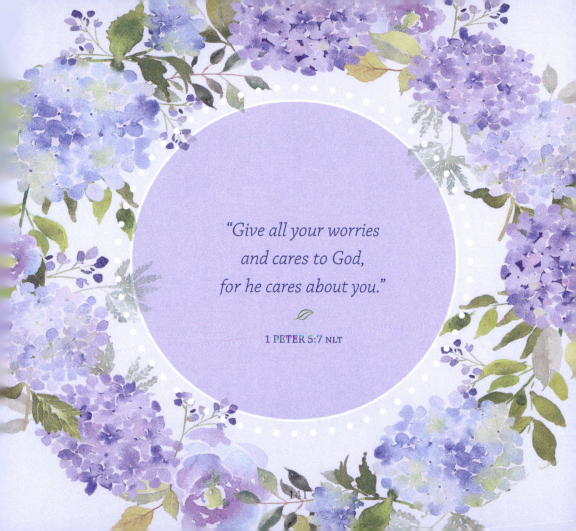

"*Give all your worries
and cares to God,
for he cares about you.*"

1 PETER 5:7 NLT

"But He gives us more and more grace [through the power of the Holy Spirit to defy sin and live an obedient life that reflects both our faith and our gratitude for our salvation]..."

JAMES 4:6

GRACE
IS NOT AN EXCUSE
TO LIVE
A SLOPPY LIFE
AND GET BY WITH IT;
IT'S THE POWER
NOT TO HAVE
TO LIVE A SINFUL LIFE.

Prayer is the greatest
privilege we have.
It's not a duty,
obligation
or last ditch effort;
it should always be
our first line of defense.

"Be unceasing in prayer
[praying perseveringly]."

1 THESSALONIANS 5:17 AMPC

THERE'S A DIFFERENCE BETWEEN
BEING BUSY AND BEING FRUITFUL.
Are you busy
or fruitful?

"...Every healthy tree
bears good fruit,
but the unhealthy tree bears bad fruit.
A good tree
cannot bear bad fruit,
nor can a bad tree bear good fruit."

MATTHEW 7:17-18

"Far from Him [all things originate]
and through Him [all things live and exist]
and to Him are all things [directed].
To Him be glory and honor forever!
Amen."

ROMANS 11:36

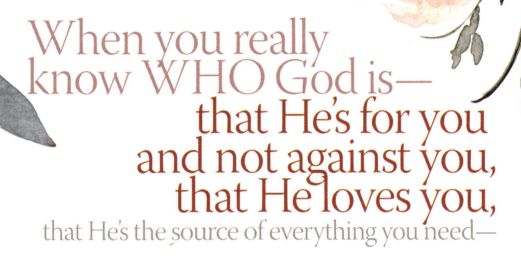

When you really
know WHO God is—
that He's for you
and not against you,
that He loves you,
that He's the source of everything you need—

then LIFE gets
really exciting!

WE GET WHAT WE BELIEVE FOR.

I'D RATHER BELIEVE FOR A LOT
AND GET HALF OF IT
THAN BELIEVE FOR NOTHING
AND GET ALL OF IT.

"For this reason I am telling you,
whatever things you ask for in prayer
[in accordance with God's will],
believe [with confident trust] that you have received them,
and they will be given to you."

MARK 11:24

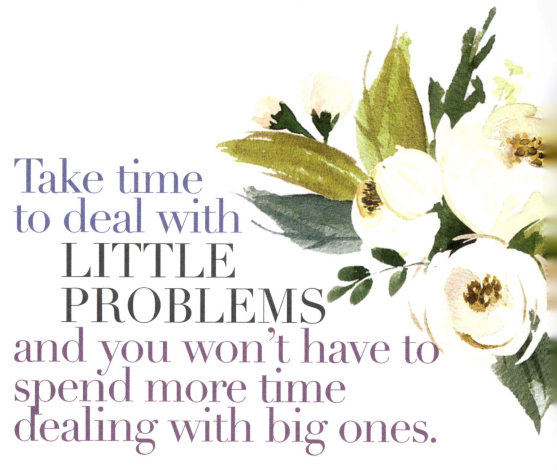

Take time
to deal with
LITTLE
PROBLEMS
and you won't have to
spend more time
dealing with big ones.

"Look carefully then
how you walk!
Live purposefully and worthily
and accurately,
not as the unwise
and witless,
but as wise
(sensible, intelligent people)."

EPHESIANS 5:15 AMPC

YOUR ABILITY TO DEFEAT STRESS IS DETERMINED BY WHAT'S GOING ON INSIDE OF YOU, NOT BY WHAT'S GOING ON OUTSIDE OF YOU IN YOUR CIRCUMSTANCES.

"A calm and undisturbed
mind and heart
are the life and health of the body,
but envy, jealousy, and wrath
are like rottenness of the bones."

PROVERBS 14:30 AMPC

"My son, do not let wisdom
and understanding out of your sight,
preserve sound judgment and discretion;
they will be life for you,
an ornament to grace your neck.
Then you will go on your way in safety,
and your foot will not stumble."

PROVERBS 3:21-23 NIV

It's what we
DO RIGHT
consistently—
OVER
AND
OVER—
that changes us.

GOD CAN
COMPLETELY
RESTORE US—
NO MATTER WHAT
WE'VE DONE
OR BEEN THROUGH.
HE WANTS TO GIVE US
DOUBLE FOR
OUR TROUBLE!

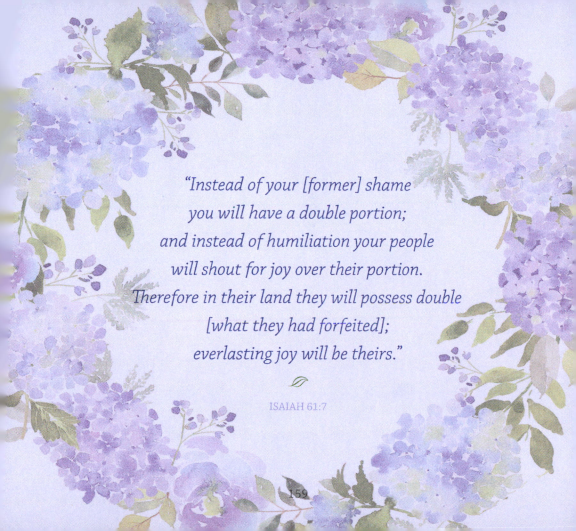

"Instead of your [former] shame
you will have a double portion;
and instead of humiliation your people
will shout for joy over their portion.
Therefore in their land they will possess double
[what they had forfeited];
everlasting joy will be theirs."

THERE IS AN ANSWER
FOR EVERY PROBLEM
IN THE WORD OF GOD.
THE BIBLE IS OUR INSTRUCTION
BOOK FOR LIFE!

*"Your word is a lamp
to my feet
and a light to my path."*

PSALM 119:105

There is no
worse life than
always being wrapped up in yourself with a
"What about me?!"
mentality.

*And He died for all,
so that all those who live might live
no longer to and for themselves,
but to and for Him Who died
and was raised again for their sake."*

2 CORINTHIANS 5:15 AMPC

Contrary to popular opinion,

YOU DON'T ALWAYS HAVE TO GIVE YOUR FEELINGS A VOTE.

Learn how to live beyond your feelings!

"For if you are living
according to the [impulses of the] flesh,
you are going to die.
But if [you are living]
by the [power of the Holy] Spirit
you are habitually putting to death
the sinful deeds of the body,
you will [really] live forever."

ROMANS 8:13

"Study and be eager and
do your utmost to present yourself
to God approved *[tested by trial]*,
a workman who has no cause to be ashamed,
correctly analyzing and accurately dividing
[rightly handling and skillfully teaching]
the Word of Truth."   2 TIMOTHY 2:15 AMPC

THE HARD THING IS
HARD FOR A REASON:
IT YIELDS
THE GREATEST
REWARD.
YOU CAN'T
HAVE THE PERKS
WITHOUT
THE WORK!

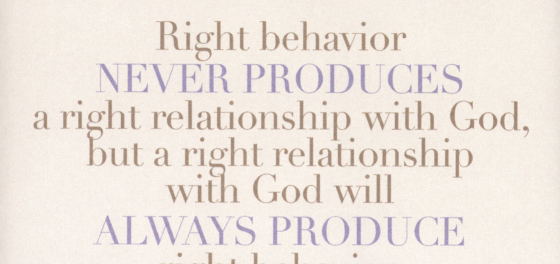

Right behavior
NEVER PRODUCES
a right relationship with God,
but a right relationship
with God will
ALWAYS PRODUCE
right behavior.

"…God is light; in him there is no darkness at all.
If we claim to have fellowship with him and yet walk
in darkness, we lie and do not live out the truth.
But if we walk in the light, as he is in the light,
we have fellowship with one another,
and the blood of Jesus, his Son,
purifies us from all sin."

1 JOHN 1:5–7 NIV

"...Jesus said,
'If you hold to my teaching,
you are really my disciples.
Then you will know the truth,
and the truth will set you free.'"

JOHN 8:31-32 NIV

Our secrets make us sick BUT God's truth sets us free!

Learn how
to live in
AGREEMENT,
even if
it means you
DISAGREE
agreeably.

"Don't have anything
to do with foolish
and stupid arguments,
because you know
they produce quarrels.
And the Lord's servant must
not be quarrelsome but must
be kind to everyone,
able to teach,
not resentful."

2 TIMOTHY 2:23-24 NIV

I love the school
of the Holy Spirit
because you never
flunk out.
You just keep
taking the test
over and over
until you pass.

"Now no chastening seems to be joyful for the present, but painful; nevertheless, afterward it yields the peaceable fruit of righteousness to those who have been trained by it."

HEBREWS 12:11 NKJV

Love is not something GOD DOES— it's who HE IS.

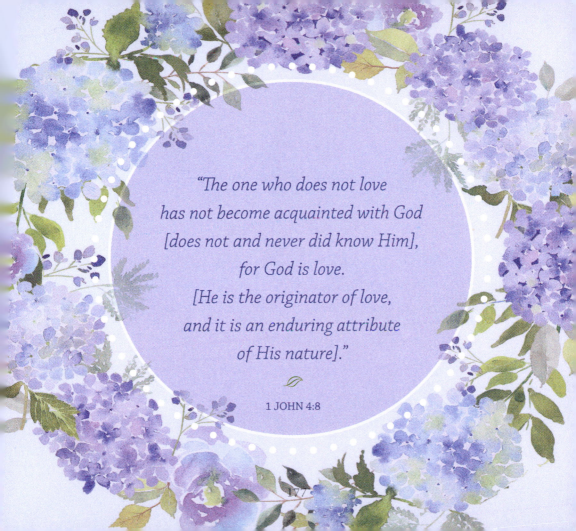

"*The one who does not love
has not become acquainted with God
[does not and never did know Him],
for God is love.
[He is the originator of love,
and it is an enduring attribute
of His nature].*"

1 JOHN 4:8

177

"...For the one who wavers
[hesitates, doubts]
is like the billowing surge out at sea
that is blown hither and thither
and tossed by the wind.
For truly, let not such a person imagine
that he will receive anything
[he asks for] from the Lord."

JAMES 1:6-7 AMPC

We have to learn how to

DOUBT OUR DOUBTS AND

MAKE A DETERMINED DECISION TO

TRUST GOD

NO MATTER HOW WE FEEL,
WHAT WE THINK OR WHAT
THE CIRCUMSTANCE LOOKS LIKE.

THERE'S NO SUCH THING AS A **DRIVE-THROUGH BREAKTHROUGH,**

AND THERE'S NO SUCH THING AS **MICROWAVE MATURITY.**

"Remain in Me, and I [will remain] in you.
Just as no branch can bear fruit by itself
without remaining in the vine,
neither can you [bear fruit,
producing evidence of your faith]
unless you remain in Me."

JOHN 15:4

EVERYONE WANTS
TO BE AN OVERCOMER

but nobody wants
to have anything
to overcome.

YOU CAN'T HAVE A TESTIMONY
WITHOUT A TEST!

*"Blessed [happy, spiritually prosperous,
favored by God] is the man who
is steadfast under trial
and perseveres when tempted;
for when he has passed the test
and been approved, he will receive
the [victor's] crown of life
which the Lord has promised to those
who love Him."*

JAMES 1:12

"In your relationships with one another,
have the same mindset as Christ Jesus:
Who, being in very nature God,
did not consider equality with God
something to be used to his own advantage;
rather, he made himself nothing
by taking the very nature of a servant,
being made in human likeness."

PHILIPPIANS 2:5-7 NIV

WE'RE NOT really free UNTIL WE'RE FREE from the need to impress OTHER PEOPLE.

*"And Abraham's faith did not weaken,
even though, at about 100 years of age,
he figured his body was as good as dead—
and so was Sarah's womb.
Abraham never wavered in believing God's promise.
In fact, his faith grew stronger,
and in this he brought glory to God.
He was fully convinced that God is able
to do whatever he promises."*

ROMANS 4:19-21 NLT

FAITH ALWAYS REQUIRES UNANSWERED QUESTIONS. IF WE KNEW EVERYTHING WE WANT TO KNOW ALL THE TIME, WE WOULDN'T NEED FAITH TO GET US THROUGH THINGS.

"And my God will
liberally supply (fill until full)
your every need
according to His riches
in glory in Christ Jesus."

PHILIPPIANS 4:19

We serve a God of
MORE THAN
ENOUGH,
not barely enough.

Don't get your "who" confused with your "do." Your true value is found when you fully understand who you are in Christ.

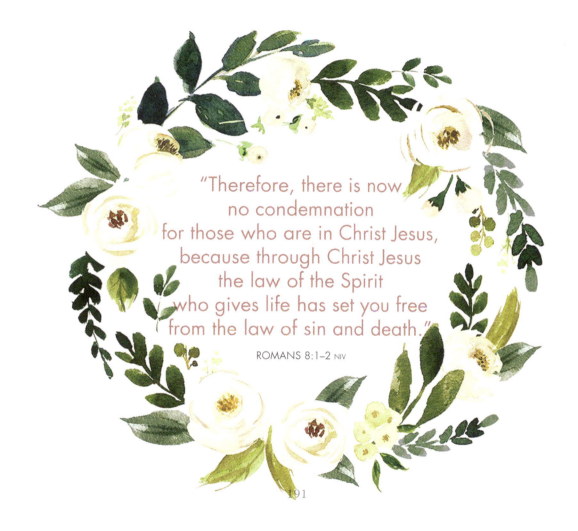

"Therefore, there is now
no condemnation
for those who are in Christ Jesus,
because through Christ Jesus
the law of the Spirit
who gives life has set you free
from the law of sin and death."

ROMANS 8:1–2 NIV

You can be
as close to God
as you want to be.
YOU JUST HAVE
TO BE WILLING
to put the time
into your relationship
with Him to get there.

*"Come near to God
and he will
come near to you..."*

JAMES 4:8 NIV

YOU CAN
BE BITTER
OR BETTER.
LET GOD USE
THE HARD THINGS
IN YOUR LIFE TO
MAKE YOU BETTER!

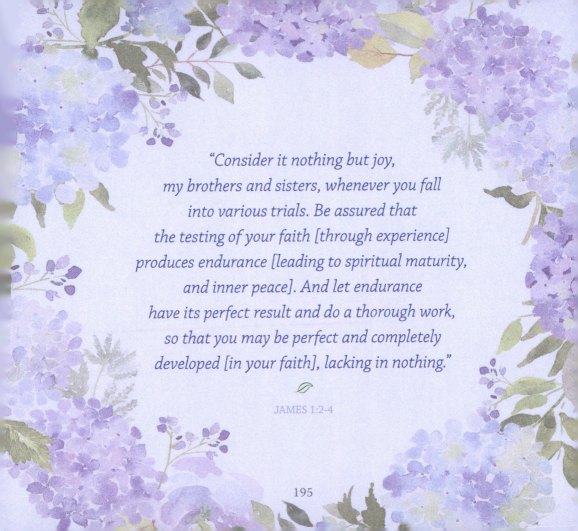

"Consider it nothing but joy,
my brothers and sisters, whenever you fall
into various trials. Be assured that
the testing of your faith [through experience]
produces endurance [leading to spiritual maturity,
and inner peace]. And let endurance
have its perfect result and do a thorough work,
so that you may be perfect and completely
developed [in your faith], lacking in nothing."

JAMES 1:2-4

Prayer changes more than things — prayer changes you!

"Pray, therefore, like this:
Our Father Who is in heaven,
hallowed (kept holy) be Your name.
Your kingdom come,
Your will be done on earth
as it is in heaven."

MATTHEW 6:9-10 AMPC

"For I want you to know, believers,
that the gospel which was preached by me
is not man's gospel [it is not a human invention,
patterned after any human concept].
For indeed I did not receive it from man,
nor was I taught it,
but I received it through
a [direct] revelation of Jesus Christ."

GALATIANS 1:11-12

We don't need more INFORMATION; we need REVELATION.

MEEKNESS
is not
WEAKNESS,
it's strength under control.

"Blessed are the meek,

for they shall inherit the earth."

MATTHEW 5:5 NKJV

"Be on guard;
stand firm in your faith
[in God, respecting His precepts
and keeping your doctrine sound].
Act like [mature] men and be courageous;
be strong."   1 CORINTHIANS 16:13

GOD HAS
GIVEN US AN
ANTIDOTE
FOR FEAR:
FAITH.
WHEN FEAR
KNOCKS
ON YOUR DOOR,
SEND FAITH
TO ANSWER.

IT'S EASY TO GIVE PEOPLE WHAT THEY DESERVE; **IT'S A PRIVILEGE** TO GIVE THEM GRACE AND MERCY.

*"Above all things
have intense and unfailing
love for one another,
for love covers a multitude of sins
[forgives and disregards
the offenses of others]."*

1 PETER 4:8 AMPC

"Fear not, for I am with you;

be not dismayed, for I am your God.

I will strengthen you, yes,

I will help you,

I will uphold you

with My righteous right hand."

ISAIAH 41:10 NKJV

COURAGE

is doing what you know
you should do
even though you feel afraid.

DO IT AFRAID!

Write a favorite
VERSE AND WHAT
IT MEANS TO YOU